W9-BCW-257

Inside
Government

LOBBYING

Cass R. Sandak

Twenty-First Century Books

A Division of Henry Holt and Company
New York

Twenty-First Century Books
A Division of Henry Holt and Company, Inc.
115 West 18th Street
New York, NY 10011

Henry Holt® and colophon are trademarks of
Henry Holt and Company, Inc.
Publishers since 1866

Library of Congress Cataloging-in-Publication Data
Sandak, Cass R.
Lobbying / Cass R. Sandak. — 1st ed.
p. cm. — (Inside government)
Includes bibliographical references (p.   ) and index.
1. Lobbying—United States—Juvenile literature. I. Title. II. Series.
JK1118.S35 1995
324'.4'0973—dc20   95–19447
                                                          CIP
                                                          AC

ISBN 0–8050–3424–2
First Edition 1995
Printed in Mexico
All first editions are printed on acid-free paper ∞.
10 9 8 7 6 5 4 3 2 1

Designed by Kelly Soong

Cover images courtesy of: U.S. Government Printing Office (flag), Public
Citizen, League of Women Voters, National Rifle Association, National
Organization For Women, American Civil Liberties Union, Greenpeace, and
Washington, D.C., Convention and Visitors Association (Capitol building).

Photo Credits
pp. 16, 20, 40, 44: The Bettmann Archive; pp. 28, 46: AP/Wide World Photos; p. 48:
David Woo/Dallas Morning News/Gamma Liaison; p. 50: J. Pat Carter/Gamma
Liaison

CONTENTS

THIS IS LOBBYING

Scenario 1

A parent-teacher organization has decided that a textbook being used in its district's school system and in other districts throughout the state contains material that many of the parents consider obscene. The parents want to employ some professionals to help them evaluate what to do. They decide to contact a group of lobbyists in Washington, D.C., that deals with educational problems.

This is lobbying.

Scenario 2

A gentleman takes a congressman to lunch. He wines and dines him in an elegant Washington restaurant. During lunch, the gentleman presents the representative with a sheaf of papers. On the papers are more than 10,000 signatures. The signatures come from concerned people in the representative's state who believe that their state's one nuclear power installation is not being run to exacting safety standards. For years many people have complained of this laxness, but the representative now has a body of signatures proving the concern. The representative knows he must do something about an issue that has been simmering quietly for a long time. He must pay attention to the unified voice he hears from his constituents.

This is lobbying.

Scenario 3

To save the troubled C-17 cargo plane project, a letter from President Bill Clinton to former House Speaker Thomas Foley circulated in the House, garnering support. In the letter, Clinton described the huge transport plane as "crucial to the Air Force's ability to deliver and sustain forces" in overseas conflicts.

The mammoth planes are expensive to build and have been subject to faults in design and huge cost overruns. But the planes are vital to Southern California's aircraft industry, where some 10,000 workers are employed in building them. The president considers the contract essential to both the economy of the area and to his own political interests in the heavily Republican region.[1]

This, too, is lobbying.

ONE
LOBBYING: WHY DO WE HAVE IT?

The verb *lobbying* comes from the noun *lobby*—a room or corridor where people wait. In many hotels or office buildings, the entrance area—sometimes a luxurious space furnished with deep, comfortable chairs—is often called the lobby. One way for a person to meet a government official whom he or she could influence is to sit and wait for the dignitary to arrive for a meeting in a place the official is likely to appear. Historically, this has been done in the halls of Congress, the corridors of legislative office buildings, and in the offices of government officials.

A recent edition of *Webster's Dictionary* defines the verb *lobby* as meaning "to conduct activities aimed at influencing public officials and especially members of a legislative body on legislation and other policy decisions."

THEORIES OF DEMOCRACY

The motto on the Great Seal of the United States is *E pluribus unum*: "out of many, one." The original reference is to a single nation, a democracy, formed out of thirteen separate colonies that became distinct states. The idea that the United States has formed one strong country out of many diverse groups of people is central to our nation's philosophy.

Pluralism is the term political theorists use to explain that in a democracy many different points of view and interests exist. These clash, compete, and work together to form our government. Everyone is entitled to be heard, but because most politically active Americans belong to more than one of many different interest groups, no single interest group predominates.

Our form of government is a representative democracy. This means that the people control the government by means of their representatives. Historically, a relationship has grown up between interest groups and legislators. It may seem strange that we need lobbying in a democracy. A whole system built around political favors and going all out to influence laws and the people who make them sounds like standard operating procedure in some foreign country. It does not seem quite American. And yet, the First Amendment—that part of America's Bill of Rights that protects free speech—constitutionally guarantees "the right of the people peaceably to assemble, and to petition the Government for a redress of grievances."

There is a difference between the way our government ought to work and the way it does work. Determination, influence, and money can sometimes derail the democratic process. There never has been (and probably never will be) a democracy where all members of society take an equal part in governing society. The reasons are many. With every person considering, debating over, and voting on every issue, nothing would ever be finished. And not everyone is capable of, or is interested in, performing the work of government.

For these and other reasons, representative government developed. The public elects professional politicians to represent them and their interests, and to perform the work of governing—making, enforcing, and interpreting laws within the framework outlined in the Constitution.

LOBBYING AS THE FOURTH BRANCH OF THE GOVERNMENT

All three branches of government are affected by lobbies and lobbyists. The number of lobbyists has grown so much in the twentieth century that lobbying is often referred to as the "fourth branch" of the U.S. government, after the executive, legislative, and judicial ones.

Executive branch: The president cannot make laws directly but can suggest new laws by working through key allies in Congress. The president often (though not always) has the power to make or break any pending piece of legislation by lending support, by gaining a majority within Congress (building a coalition), or by exercising presidential veto power. The president may lobby for an important issue or project and may enlist friends and supporters to do the same. Because of this pivotal position, the president is a prime target for lobbyists.

Legislative branch: Lobbyists provide a valuable service in that they bring information on issues to the attention of legislators and other members of the legislative branch. In fact, they often bombard members of government with facts and statistics. However, the information provided by lobbyists most often reflects a strong bias and may be incomplete or even inaccurate.

Judicial branch: Particular lobbies, for example women's groups or civil rights lobbyists, may have their own choices for the candidates who will fill key judicial posts. Lobbies may press for particular Supreme Court appointments or support the election or appointment of lower court judges. Lobbyists may also try to sway public opinion in both higher and lower court decisions. Certainly the interests of vocal minorities have helped shape Supreme Court decisions on such issues as abortion rights and prayer in the public schools.

THE PRECEDENT FOR LOBBIES

The building blocks of a democratic society include many interest groups. It is simply not possible for each individual to take an active role in government. That is not the same as saying the individual is powerless. It simply means that the role that most citizens play is restricted to voting—unless they are engaged in the work of lobbying to influence the making and enforcement of laws.

The three largest segments of the U.S. economy—labor, agriculture, and manufacturing—lobby on a regular basis. In addition, smaller groups, such as those representing medical doctors or attorneys, can have remarkable influence on laws and government policy. These people represent highly affluent and articulate groups. Other interest groups include churches, bankers, educators, real estate agents, motorcyclists, dairy farmers—you name it. In fact, a study has shown that only about 25 percent of the U.S. population is not represented by one or more interest groups.[1] And no one can escape the impact of interest groups and their lobbying efforts.

ONE GOVERNMENT: MANY DIFFERENT VOICES

Lobbying gives representation to the factions in American society and indirectly provides average citizens with a powerful voice. Members of Congress may actually rely on lobbyists to get the information they need to keep themselves and their constituents well informed. Special interest lobbies work actively on environmental issues, highway safety, public health, and the reform of government itself.

There are always play-offs between the conflicting demands of interest groups with radically different agendas. The president and members of Congress are regularly pulled in different directions. It is a constant moral dilemma to ensure that it is not just the side that has the most money that always wins.

Lobbying is the forum wherein the facets of diverse issues may be explored from every possible viewpoint, both for and against. Women's rights, reproductive freedom, gay and lesbian rights, censorship, gun control, and substance use and abuse are just some of the important issues that engage today's lobbyists.

The terms *lobbies*, *interest groups*, and *pressure groups* are sometimes used interchangeably, though of course the degree of pressure brought by different groups varies enormously depending on numbers of people, the money available, the skill of the lobbyists, and the merits of their message.

Lobbying is one of the realities of political life that may not appear pleasant, but it is good to remember that individuals and organizations can lobby for worthwhile ends. Increased funding for education is for the benefit of society. Lobbying for copyright laws to protect authors, musicians, and others from having their work pirated is also a just cause.

Lobbying is a tool that can give individuals more clout—the power to influence legislation by joining up with other groups and individuals who share the same lobbying interests. Lobbies allow minorities, who are generally underrepresented in government, a chance to have their needs addressed and listened to.

Lobbying goes beyond voting in empowering people to influence their government. Because it is such an ingrained part of the structure of government, it can give power to people, such as foreigners, who may not even be enfranchised to vote. Lobbying opens the door to "outside" interests—businesses in one state or region can sway legislation in other states or regions where they may have no right to vote. Foreign governments may use lobbyists to secure aid monies, treaties, trade agreements, technology exchange programs, military help, and even goodwill. These are just some of the ways that foreign governments can use our government to promote their own interests.

LOBBYING'S PAST

Forms of lobbying predate the actual founding of the United States. The practice goes back in history to a time when kings and noblemen held court and subjects approached them seeking justice and the redress of certain wrongs. In the same way, people have often traveled great distances and endured hardships to speak with an influential person, a member of a king's court, or a powerful church official to get help with a special problem.

Early colonists "lobbied" (although the word was not in use then) for attention. John Adams and Samuel Adams were courted in Revolutionary days by citizens who wanted to influence the new government's rulings regarding trade and taxes. The new country's first tariff act (a tax on imported goods) was passed in 1789, and American lobbying—much as we know it today—began about that time.[1]

In the *Federalist Papers*, James Madison talked about private and special interests. He called them factions. Madison was concerned about keeping a balance between the needs of different interest groups. He wanted to keep factions from forming so that the government and the people all would form one union of effort. But for a long time, people have had a hard time distinguishing between their own good and the good of the many.

Following the War of 1812, mill owners in the North sought to boost New England's cotton textile industry by demanding tariffs that favored their region and its industry, even though cheaper cloth was available from Britain.

Lobbying as a term for political influence-seeking appears to have been used for the first time around 1829 in Albany, the capital of New York State. People trying to influence state politicians were seen around Albany's capitol building, looking to favor their own regions or businesses. They were known then as "lobby-agents." By the 1830s, the term *lobbyist* was in general use, and the term had spread to Washington, D.C., the nation's capital.

WHERE DOES THE NAME LOBBYING COME FROM?

There is a legend, perhaps not true, that Washington, D.C.'s, famed Willard Hotel was the source of the word *lobbying*. Seekers of political favors would prowl the hotel's elegant lobby in search of a government official with a sympathetic ear. The first Willard Hotel was built around 1818; the present building dates from 1901. Since the hotel is only a few short blocks from the White House, the story may indeed be true.

LOBBYING GETS A BAD NAME

Through much of history, lobbying has had a dirty name. In the mid-nineteenth century, the American economy was growing rapidly, but there was no income tax, there were no unions, and there were no child labor laws. It was the age of "robber barons," rich men whose money could buy anything. The great railroads, which transformed America from coast to coast in the nineteenth century, were built on land that for the most part had been acquired illegally.

By the mid-nineteenth century, a lobbyist was considered a crook and a devious person bent on influencing politicians even if corruption was involved. And it usually was. In the eyes of most people, a lobbyist was a subhuman form of individual.

The financial panic of 1857 also helped contribute to lobbying's bad reputation. Lobbyists representing bankers, brokers, real estate interests, et cetera, barged into the offices of Washington's legislators. By and large, they were dishonest people who would stoop to blackmail and bribery to achieve their desired ends. They wanted to get laws changed to protect the moneymen and their fortunes rather than the interests of common people who had invested their life savings.

During the Reconstruction period after the Civil War, a disillusioned country provided many openings for wrongdoing. Political patronage (whereby politicians—especially senators—handed out civil service posts to their supporters and other favorites) and the "spoils system" were standard practice. Under the spoils system, officials elected to posts lorded over their districts as if they were the spoils of war.

By the late nineteenth century, lobbying had reached its height of power and its depth of corruption. Lobbyists for the railroads and other industrial interests regularly sought outright favors from state legislators. They bought votes in state legislatures and even in Congress. President James Garfield fought for reform in the corrupt patronage system but paid for his efforts with his life. In 1881 he was assassinated by an anarchist who was also a disappointed office seeker.

At the turn of the century, the power of corporations and trusts was largely uncurbed. Muckraking journalists made their shocking exposures of industry's abuses against workers. Public investigations into these instances helped bring about the enactment of laws to protect the public.

Since 1910, congressional investigations have cracked down on charges of favoritism against public officeholders in awarding political appointments. Outright abuse has become impossible. But lobbies are still heavy contributors to the campaign funds of elected officials. This still leaves room for political favors and the appearance of misconduct.

There have always been whistle-blowers who have tried to

clean up instances of political abuse. Senator Robert M. La Follette of Wisconsin was a leader of the antilobby movement in Congress in the early twentieth century. He wanted to bring the activities of lobbyists out in the open, making them more subject to scrutiny by the public and analysis in the press. He argued that "every legal argument which any lobbyist has to

---

MUCKRAKING

In the nineteenth century, newspapers began to emerge as a powerful force helping to shape society. *Muckraking* is a term for the kind of courageous journalism that emerged. Far more than scandalmongering (trying to sell more papers by reporting shameful and scandalous doings of the rich and powerful), reporters and editors sought social and political reform by bringing to light what was really going on in political and business life. For example, the corrupt world of New York City politics and Boss Tweed was one focus of early muckraking efforts, especially by cartoonist Thomas Nast.

Today the muckraking tradition continues in the type of reporting practiced by many newspapers, especially the *New York Times* and the *Washington Post*, and by broadcast journalists and such TV programs as *60 Minutes* and *20/20*.

---

offer, and which any legislator ought to hear, can be presented before committees, before the legislature as a body, through the press, from the public platform, and through printed briefs and arguments placed in the hands of all members and accessible to the public."[2] La Follette and others like him tried to end the kind of politics that takes place behind closed doors, out of public view.

☆ ═══════ ☆

*Carrie Nation, the woman with the hatchet, was caricatured for
her famous destruction of Noble's painting of* Cleopatra at the Bath.

Following World War I, organizations to promote the public welfare through peace societies, veterans' groups, and other
types of social alliances for the first time became a larger force in
lobbying than private business interests. These groups were the
forerunners of today's public interest lobbies such as Common
Cause and the League of Women Voters (see chapter 5).

Surely one of the longest-lasting lobbying efforts in
American history has been the one surrounding the legality of
selling alcoholic beverages. Two of the strongest lobbyists against
liquor were Carrie Nation and Wayne Bidwell Wheeler. Nation
was a colorful extremist who believed that alcohol was evil. She
often carried an ax into saloons and chopped up bars gleefully.
Wheeler founded the Anti-Saloon League. He organized a

march on Washington in 1913, and almost single-handedly was responsible for the proposal of the Eighteenth Amendment by Congress.[3] Passed in 1920, and commonly known as the Prohibition Amendment, it banned the sale of all liquor.

The Prohibition amendment was repealed in 1933, but the damage had been done: all kinds of illegal trade in alcoholic beverages and underground racketeering began during this period, and although Prohibition has been finished for more than sixty years, the legacy of corruption and organized crime lives on. Lobbyists continue to press for stricter laws controlling advertising of alcoholic beverages, higher age limits for legal drinking, and tougher laws against drunk drivers and permissible blood alcohol levels.

Since the 1930s, there has been a decline in the effectiveness of direct lobbying by these special interest groups on both national and state levels. The Depression period saw a shift away from private interests toward legislation designed to benefit the majority. The 1930s and 1940s were the era of President Franklin D. Roosevelt's New Deal, and lobbyists on behalf of labor unions were numerous, powerful, and conspicuous.

REGULATION HELPS CLEAN UP LOBBYING'S IMAGE

Major legislative developments began to work against the power of business lobbies. The year 1934 saw the end of certain tariff measures and the rise of reciprocal trade agreements, which countered regionalism and protectionism. President Roosevelt actually had lobbyists on his payroll. He used them to influence Congress to pass the bills he favored.

In an effort to curtail the bribery that was part of so much lobbying, Congress passed the Legislative Reorganization Act in 1946. One section of the act is called the Federal Reorganization of Lobbying Act. This act requires that lobbyists must register with the clerk of the House of Representatives and the secretary of the Senate. Such legislation at state and national levels has brought the work of lobbyists out in the open. No longer can lobbyists do their work secretly, unobserved by the public and news media. The watchdog function of responsible journalism and the accountability to the government have helped to curb the abusive practices of lobbyists. This registration has helped to clean up lobbying's image.

Federal and state laws regulating lobbying have pretty much kept lobbyists' activities aboveboard and legal and stopped the exchange of much "under-the-table" money. The flaw is that the regulations apply only to a lobbyist who is being paid. The law also applies to a person whose "principal purpose" is lobbying, and that's a tough one to prove or even define, since lobbying can occur in subtle ways on different levels.

Since 1962, as part of the Kennedy administration's tax reform package, money spent by individuals, businesses, and groups on lobbying efforts has been tax deductible. This means that at the same time that individuals or groups are spending money to promote their own interests, they are also reducing their tax burden. However, such tax advantages are changing now with the lobbying reform initiative spearheaded by President Clinton and Congress.

Despite regulation, improper lobbying has not ended. The most recent decades in congressional history are filled with cases of unethical behavior by legislators. Incredibly, even following censure in Congress, many of these individuals have been reelected to further terms.

During the Reagan administration, there was a marked shift toward the seamier side of lobbying. More than one hundred high-level members of that president's administration had charges leveled against them for illegal or unethical practices in lobbying. Other individuals with high-level government connections—friends of Reagan as well as friends and relatives of George Bush—sailed through major economic upheavals like the savings and loan crisis and insider trading scandals virtually unscathed.

THREE
CAMPAIGNING
FOR VOTES

History shows that lobbying springs from a checkered past. But by and large, the day of the crooked, self-interested lobbyist is over. Today lobbies function on a wider scale and are more professional than ever before. Modern lobbying takes place at local, state, and federal levels. Because of this large-scale involvement, lobbying is an important force that shapes all levels of government. More than 2,500 lobbying groups have their headquarters in Washington, D.C., to be near the seat of our government. Many more groups are spread throughout the country, mostly in larger cities and state capitals.

The organizations that lobbyists represent in Washington run the gamut from hard-nosed business giants to well-meaning philanthropies, from trade unions, professional associations, and labor organizations to private interests, from particular state and city governments around the nation to the governments of foreign countries. The groups that seek access and influence in the federal arena include churches and other religious groups, chambers of commerce, and recreational groups.

The cachet of celebrity names can help bring extra attention to a cause. The late Jacqueline Kennedy Onassis lobbied on behalf of architectural preservation at the state and city levels. Mrs. Onassis believed strongly that New York City's Grand Central Station, threatened with destruction, was an important New York Landmark.

There are lobbies for increasing funds for research into AIDS or breast cancer; there are lobbies to save endangered species; there are lobbies to protect endangered wetlands; there are lobbies to save buildings in danger of crumbling and museums and libraries in danger of closing. There are lobbies that represent real estate agencies, tavern owners, the elderly, and the sick.

Basically there are two paths open to lobbyists: the legal and the illegal. An example of lobbying the correct way might be giving testimony before a congressional committee or providing informational pamphlets to members of Congress. Less desirable methods occur privately and are therefore not always subject to public scrutiny. They might include personal meetings and interviews or scheduled events such as luncheons, dinners, or galas. At these functions, lobbyists may buttonhole key government figures and barrage them with attention intended to sway their opinions. At the bottom end of the scale is out-and-out bribery—corrupt, illegal, unattractive, and definitely

Security officers endeavor to remove a demonstrator during President Bush's speech to the National Leadership Coalition on AIDS.

against the law. Still, there are gray areas of how much and what legislators can in conscience accept from lobbyists.

LOBBYING AND LEGISLATORS

The legislators—the people who make state or federal laws—are the most important targets of lobbyists. Lobbying can affect the passage of legislation favorable to a particular group. It can also influence the way the government spends public monies (which is done by legislation, either by increasing appropriations or by cutting back on programs). The repeal of taxes that seem to fall unfairly on a single group as well as the imposition of trade tariffs against foreign competition may be influenced by lobbyists.

Groups pay lobbyists to influence legislators in the way laws are made and to present the issues that form the need for these laws. Strong lobbying usually takes place whenever a proposed law is controversial. It may also occur when the law will affect a lot of people or when taxpayers will end up paying a lot of money.

Lobbyists and lobbies seek to influence both legislative and administrative decisions. They exert an influence disproportionate to their numbers. Lobbyists could never hope to gain majority support in a general election. They may endorse and lend support to a favored candidate, but they do not nominate their own candidates. They try to work with the candidates who are elected from either party, and they usually confine their agendas to a single issue or set of related issues.

Lobbies are sometimes referred to as pressure groups. *Pressure* may seem like too strong a word for a lobbyist's intent; yet lobbying is more than the neutral transmission of information. The information that lobbyists provide may be strongly biased. Lobbyists try hard to influence lawmakers. At the same time, lawmakers are being influenced by other forces. Legislators take their cues from their parties, the president, their colleagues, and their constituents, in addition to other loyalties and sources, including the media and voters in general.

Lobbying is a way that individuals or interest groups communicate with their congresspeople. If a grassroots lobbyist can collect 25,000 signatures on a petition asking for certain legislation, for example, the member of Congress must sit up and, at the very least, take notice of this large number of voters who support a certain cause. To ignore the demands of potential voters could be a costly political mistake come election time.

Studies have demonstrated that the impact of lobbying is often overstated. Legislators have other sources of information besides lobbyists. Values, personal integrity, and constituent needs are also of paramount importance.

Legislators like to have it both ways. They are the willing recipients of the lobbyists' largess, such as gifts and entertainment. On the other hand, with their constituencies they strongly profess independence when defending their judgments. For some legislators, the conflict of interests—the pull between serving the needs of their constituents and enjoying the rewards offered by lobbyists—presents a moral dilemma. The very conflict has led to the need for reform within the lobbying system.

INTEREST GROUPS

Interest groups concentrate their efforts on two fronts. They influence public opinion by building public awareness and sympathy. Spreading an idea makes it harder to ignore. Secondly, interest groups direct media attention (possibly even engineering events that will underscore their claim) in order to influence legislators.

Interest groups can be large or small, rich or poor. Sporting goods manufacturers and cable television networks are just two examples of interest groups. Their needs may be of little concern to most of the world, or they may affect the lives of just about everyone. Lobbyists who represent business interest groups supply information relating to conditions in a certain industry. They talk and argue with individual legislators and testify before government committees. The need for safety regulations at rock concerts is an issue that has just recently come to the attention of lawmakers. Hearings in Congress usually occur before a bill is voted on, so lobbyists often provide formal testimony and plead their cases before legislators at this time. Sometimes members of Congress (and even the president) need extra support to get enough votes for a bill they want passed. They may actually enlist lobbyists to persuade others to adopt their viewpoints. In this way, they can target other legislators and help sway public opinion. President Clinton used this tactic in gaining support for the passage of the NAFTA and GATT trade agreements that he favored.

A new phenomenon is the so-called grassroots connection. Lobbyists are, after all, the people who feel they know the issues and "what the folks back home are thinking." Sometimes congresspeople need this kind of local connection to keep them in touch with the realities of public feeling about an issue.

WHO AND WHAT ARE THE MOST SUCCESSFUL LOBBIES?

It would be safe to say that the corporate giants under the control of America's business elite may not be the most numerous but are among the most successful interest groups influencing the state and federal government's legislative branch. They manipulate public opinion through public relations and advertising campaigns, through media control, and by rallying grassroots support through saturation efforts such as telephone calls and letter writing. A recent article in *Time* magazine noted that "the trend today is to 'grass-roots lobbying'—that is, influencing legislators by stirring up a storm of letters and phone calls from their constituents back home."[1]

The power elite largely control the country's legislative agenda by devoting large sums of money to lobbying efforts. As William Domhoff, an authority on American government writes, "What the studies show is that most lobbying is done by business associations and that they are most effective when their intent is to block legislation rather than create it."[2] Usually, such business interests also seek control of the regulatory agencies. They achieve this by influencing political appointments and by carefully orchestrating elections with massive campaign contributions. And the flow of money continues after the elections; the balls and banquets that surround the inaugurations of new presidents, governors, and the swearing-in ceremonies of other officials are often funded by lobbying interests.

Big business may dominate the lobbying scene, but smaller interest groups that represent powerful organizations of professionals (e.g., the American Medical Association and the Association of Trial Lawyers of America) can also have clout disproportionate to their numbers. In short, these groups have the power of dollars. It is difficult to believe that all of these interest groups are working for the common good. Many of them are not. The AMA has worked to limit the number of physicians. The ATLA has fought efforts to contain legal costs.

It is also likely that in the future interest groups and lobbying will have an even larger role to play in American political life, particularly as other sources of campaign funds dry up. The money that goes to fill up campaign chests comes less and less from individual contributors and more and more from large, powerful organizations.

LOBBYING IN EDUCATION

School curricula have become more and more a battleground for lobbyists. The courses taught, textbooks used, and ideals and values represented have most certainly been shaped by lobbying and lobbyists.

Lobbyists turned the issue of prayer in the classroom into a tug-of-war between the religious right and the liberal left. Lobbyists have argued over school building safety standards regarding safe levels of lead and asbestos. Lobbying is behind what is taught, including such issues as cultural diversity, informing young people of health dangers through AIDS education, and balancing evolutionary theory with the teaching of creation science.

Lobbyists directly affect the content of textbooks that publishers prepare. Publishers know their books will never sell in certain states or individual school districts if they do not furnish material that is consistent with the agendas of the political forces in the states where their books will be marketed. The lobbying forces basically represent the beliefs of conservative parent groups. But now liberal groups such as the American Civil Liberties Union, are entering the fray to give voice to less traditional viewpoints.

LOBBYING IN CONTROL OF THE CLASSROOM

The length of the school year—roughly ten months, with a ten-week summer vacation—originated in an agrarian society, when students were needed to help on the farm during growing season and harvest. But today the reasons for the traditional calendar have shifted. Hard as it is to believe, the length of the school year—180 days through most of the United States—has largely been determined by a lobby supported by amusement park owners who fear a dramatic loss in revenue if the school year were to be extended into the summer months.

LOBBYING AND NETWORKING

Lobbying is more than just arguing an issue. Lobbyists often build lifelong relationships with legislators. Much of lobbyists' influence is built upon "friendships" formed with legislators who can help the interest groups' gain an ear. These relationships can be of critical importance at some pivotal point—as when a particularly important bill is about to be voted on. Sometimes lobbies also can provide a legal second source of income for legislators by offering hefty fees for speeches given before meetings of lobbying group members or the public.

Lobbying can affect legislation during any stage of a bill's life from its inception to its time "in committee," when legislators hear arguments about the proposed legislation by other legislators, by expert witnesses called in to testify, and by citizens concerned about the bill's passage. Lobbyists may intervene with an information campaign and other senators may introduce bills that compete with the objectives of the bill under consideration.

Often lobbyists try to kill a bad or unfavorable bill by urging lawmakers to vote against it. They can present nightmare scenarios: "If that bill is passed, 100,000 people will lose their jobs." Lobbyists may try to sway legislators by simply threatening to withdraw campaign financial support.

Or lobbyists may press for a more favorable compromise bill. The compromise system guarantees that everyone gets something of what they want, even if it is not everything they had hoped for. Environmentalists lobbying to preserve a wilderness area might be satisfied with this compromise: "If we can't stop the logging industry from disfiguring this forest, we'll confine them to just this area." The president, responding to a delegation of mayors from flood-ravaged cities who are asking for federal aid, might respond, "We can't send flood victims $4 billion in disaster relief, but we can provide $2 billion." Compromise is a political maneuver of give-and-take.

BEING PREPARED: GATHERING AND USING INFORMATION

Lobbyists must do their homework. They must know *both* sides of their issue. If they favor a bill, they want to present the "pro" sides in the most persuasive way possible. And knowing the "cons," or opposing viewpoints, is just as important, so that they can effectively counter them. The ground rules are similar to those used in debating.

Part of being prepared means understanding the factors that led to the current situation. Perhaps a current law has its basis in some nineteenth-century scandal; it may have been passed to prevent some abuse that is no longer a political reality. Understanding this context can help lobbyists when they build a strategy. Effective lobbyists need to get to know the legislators and their voting records. The study of vote taking in Congress and roll call analysis provide interesting data on the way individuals, parties, and coalitions have voted in the past. This information helps one to understand how the legislative process depends on the responses of particular individuals.

Lobbyists can gather information from libraries, specialist societies, lectures, meetings, experts, articles in newspapers and journals, and organizations. Some public interest groups—for example, the League of Women Voters—exist for the primary purpose of gathering and sharing information.

Lobbyists should be well acquainted with the government's directories of information. The *Congressional Record* is a transcript of the transactions of the sessions of Congress, published daily and bound in volumes periodically. The *Congressional Record* can be a source of information about the testimony given by lobbyists to congressional committees. Lobbyists should also read newspapers carefully (especially the *New York Times*, the *Wall Street Journal*, and the *Washington Post*) and keep files of key news clippings. Local newspapers and magazines can also be important sources of information about political situations, business trends, labor or industrial problems, public opinion, special needs, and a host of other issues.

LOBBYISTS AS PRESENTERS OF INFORMATION

The work of representing the needs of special interest groups in Washington goes *beyond* simple lobbying—that is, trying to persuade certain legislators to vote a certain way. It is a whole field of "government relations" and information management. Through informational mailings, direct meetings and interviews, receptions, and dinners, lobbyists try to change the ways that legislators think and feel about their causes—making converts to a new point of view.

Press releases to the media are one way to sway public opinion, but press kits targeted for use by members of the legislature also may need to be prepared. The content of these kits may include newspaper or magazine articles, video- and audiotape presentations, or electronic CD-ROM material. Editorials and strategically placed news items in influential newspapers or wide-circulation magazines can help sway public opinion as well as the opinions of legislators.

Photo opportunities hark back to a more innocent time in American political life. Examples might include the time-honored tradition of a politician glad-handing well-wishers or kiss-

A "Peace Fleet" protest shows a motorized dinghy bearing a Greenpeace banner against nuclear weapons.

ing a baby. Or a legislator and spouse might be shown breaking a bottle of champagne against the hull of a new submarine as a way of showing how defense money is being spent.

A direct type of media assault includes scheduling press conferences—question-and-answer sessions between the press and prominent legislators or lobbyists. Reactions to media events that favor opposing views should promptly be put forth in the press or on TV. Lobbying state governors (or their spouses) can often be an effective tactic in securing high-level allies and potential mouthpieces for special causes.

Lobbyists need to be clever at "manufacturing" news. Staging public demonstrations and protest marches can help bring the lobbyist's message into the realm of daily news coverage. Citizens' marches on Washington, D.C., by dairy farmers, by supporters of AIDS research or nuclear disarmament, and by workers for gay and lesbian rights fall into this category.

APPROACHING LEGISLATORS DIRECTLY

Lobbyists need to sit in on congressional committee meetings. Committees are the working units where much of the power to make or break proposed legislation resides. Lobbyists will probably schedule personal visits with legislators. These require strict management, and lobbyists must put the best face on themselves and their issues.

Letters can be very effective; they can be thoughtful and provocative and leave an indelible paper trail. Telephone calls are not, however, the best method: there is no record of the calls, they are easy to ignore, and the possibility of creating misunderstandings is there. Still, they *can* be an effective part of a quickly mounted grassroots effort to show broad-based support for an issue.

Lobbyists go all out to court their targeted legislators. No favor is too extravagant. Impossible-to-get tickets to top theatrical or sporting events, lavish vacation trips (often referred to as "fact-finding missions"), suites of furniture, objects of art, and expensive jewelry have all found their way into the hands of senators or representatives considered key players in the struggle to obtain favorable treatment or legislation. Admiral Hyman Rickover, father of the naval nuclear program, and his wife were favorites of the defense industry. But they are thought to have accepted more gifts from defense contractors than they ought to have. It is little wonder that from time to time members of Congress face accusations of bribery and sometimes undergo investigation and trial on charges of unethical behavior.

THE NEGATIVE SIDE OF LOBBYING

Much of the negative feeling that the term *lobbyist* may arouse is well deserved. Certainly lobbying is an area of government that has been fraught with abuse—and the potential for overstepping the bounds of law or of ethics is always present.

Lobbying can express a limited or extremist point of view. Obviously lobbyists present the needs of their interest group. They work doggedly for what is best in the eyes of their interest group, not necessarily what is best for the country as a whole or for society in general.

Probably the most pernicious lobbying is done secretly by corporations that apply vast resources to influencing legislation in their favor, regardless of the public good. Often this goes to the extent of suppressing unfavorable information that might be disclosed through the publication of scientific investigative data (e.g., the smoking lobby).

Because of the potential for abuse, many states have enacted laws to regulate lobbying activities. These laws require lobbyists to register with a state lobbying agency affiliated with the state attorney general's office. Some laws also bar lobbyists from presence in legislative chambers except when appearing before committees. Registration includes such details as name of the lobbyist and employer (and business), salary, and details of the amounts being spent on lobbying by the business interest.

LOBBYING IS BIG BUSINESS

Today there are more than 15,000 professional lobbyists at work in Washington. Many of these lobbyists are the heads of labor unions or professional associations, organization chiefs, and corporate representatives headquartered in the nation's capital. Nearly 5,000 of these 15,000 lobbyists are special consultants—lawyers and government relations experts employed by special lobbying firms.

The numbers seem to suggest that legislators are tremendously outnumbered by lobbyists, approximately thirty to one. But this is a false picture. We must recognize that the legislative branch, in addition to the elected members of Congress, employs more than 30,000 other people—aides, staffers, and administrative assistants. These people are often deeply involved in the lawmaking process and are also subject to lobbying pressure. Busy lawmakers delegate much of their business—research, correspondence, telephone calls, attending receptions—to their assistants.

Much of the vast amount of information provided by lobbyists is sifted through and evaluated by staff members, who weigh the data so that an objective view can be obtained. Members of Congress are usually the final evaluators of the merits of an issue presented by lobbyists. But often they respond to the recommendations of their own staff members, who have reported on the lobbyists' information campaign.

LOBBYING AS A PROFESSION

For the vast majority of lobbyists, lobbying is simply a business—something they get paid to do. And of course it makes sense for them to do it well and honestly. Their agenda is *professional* rather than personal or even political. Their one goal is to achieve the ends sought by their group. Like the work of representative government itself, lobbying is a practical necessity. Lobbyists are well paid; the largest chunk of money spent on lobbying goes to pay lobbyists' salaries.

By law, only about half the money actually spent by lobbying groups needs to be reported. Because of the way the laws are written, only money spent to directly influence pending legislation is actually required to be reported. In many ways, this can open the door for abuse. Lobbies spend vast amounts in "courting" legislators through lavish dinners, lunches, receptions, banquets, and other "benefit" type functions. As journalists in *Time* magazine note, there are "difficulties in defining what is and is not lobbying that plague enforcement of the law requiring lobbyists to register."[5]

Lobbyists can pour money into "setting legislators up"—creating lots of goodwill and perhaps even a slight feeling of obligation. The groundwork has been laid so that perhaps in another year or two the particular key lawmakers will be positioned to vote favorably for the lobbyists' interests. For example, a certain industrial giant might hold a lease on the mineral rights to certain federal lands. In a few years, when the lease comes up for renewal, a senator who has been treated well by company representatives may be inclined to do all in his power not to disappoint his good friends at the mining company.

Lobbyists for a certain industry or interest may be in a position to learn innocently (or not so innocently) that the federal or state government plans to embark in the future on a search for a new federal contractor to supply fiber-optic cable or a new type of all-terrain vehicle for use by the armed forces or that new standards for automotive emissions may be introduced. This insider information can give businesspeople an edge that may prove profitable. The money invested in lobbying has been well spent and can go unreported because it was not directed toward a particular legislative goal.

LOBBYIST PROFILE

Many of the most effective lobbyists have been recruited from the ranks of former government officials. The House Armed Services Committee conducted a survey that found that more than 1,400 former officers in the armed services (including 261 army or air force generals and naval admirals) upon retirement from the military had taken jobs as lobbyists with top defense contractors. In their new jobs, their duty is to press for additional defense contracts for their new employers.[6]

Corporate lobbyists are usually attorneys and/or former members of Congress. Because of their training and experience, they are uniquely familiar with the workings of legislative procedure. Their personal contacts make it easy to keep tabs on the legislative agendas of both the Senate and the House. They know the precise moment to apply a little pressure, a last-minute cajole just when a bill is about to be voted on. Even when their methods are completely legal and aboveboard, such tactics can lead to an undue influence over the entire lawmaking process.

One attribute of an effective lobbyist—particularly with respect to a controversial issue that might later resurface in an unfortunate light such as an ugly lawsuit or a political scandal—is anonymity. It is desirable for lobbyists to keep a low profile, not to be too much in the limelight. This is especially important when leaking information to the press.

One of the enigmas of lobbying is the *way* important decisions are made. They are largely the result of encounters that take place behind closed doors rather than publicly, in the political forum. It is hard to regulate what happens in private. And the American public is left with a government that is largely prey to forces that the people cannot see, actions and events that they are unable to control or even to assess.

CITIZEN LOBBYISTS

Lobbying is not the exclusive bailiwick of the professional lobbyist. Lobbying is the constitutional right of every citizen to influence legislation. And the citizen lobbyist is and should be a force to contend with both at the federal and state levels. Citizen lobbyists may be more committed and more effective than those who are merely doing it for a living.

A citizen lobbyist needs to assess what he or she can do by linking up with like-minded individuals and organizations. Social groups or similar organizations may be a good place to start. Many groups lobby by organizing bus trips that bring scores of committed voters to Washington, D.C., or to their state capital to present their views.

FOUR
FOREIGN LOBBIES

Money talks; money channeled through lobbying efforts gives access to American lawmakers to foreign nationals who rightfully have no voice in American political life. *New York Times* journalists Steven Engelberg and Martin Tolchin have noted that: "For generations, foreign governments and companies from South America to East Asia have hired high-powered Washington lobbyists to press their views on their friends in government. In many cases, this is still true."[1] Foreign nationals and the lobbyists employed by them can have a profound effect on the foreign policy of the U.S. government. This situation may not always be desirable.

THE CHINA LOBBY

Foreign policy is often determined by lobbyists, although it is, in fact, supposed to be set by the president and secretary of state, in conjunction with the Senate.

In the mid-1950s, the China lobby determined to disavow any knowledge of Communist China and spent untold dollars and time trying to convince Americans that the only "true" Chinese government was run by President Chiang Kai-shek from the island of Taiwan. This policy lasted from 1949 until President Richard M. Nixon's visit to mainland China in 1972. A great deal of the money the United States had given Chiang was channeled by him back into America's China lobby to create the illusion in the United States that he had a strong chance of resuming leadership in mainland China. There wasn't actually much hope of this, but the lobby tried to convince most Americans that it was a strong possibility. During much of this period, America was violently anti-Communist, so the time was right for such a strong denial of political reality.

Finally, in 1971, the United Nations spearheaded a realistic acceptance of the politcal situation and allowed Communist China to become a member of the organization. What the world had long recognized—that Communist China was going to be around for a while longer—became a reality.

THE ISRAEL LOBBY

The American Israel Public Affairs Committee (AIPAC) is a well-organized lobby with a simple, single-minded cause— gaining U.S. support of Israel. The lobby is the most powerful and successful policy-making force in America's relations with the Middle East. Because of the lobby's efforts, nearly half the members of both houses of Congress consistently support Israel.

The organization does not directly give campaign contributions but coordinates the political campaign gifts of the more than seventy pro-Israel political action committees (PACs) that exist in this country. The group also coordinates the work of hundreds of other Jewish organizations in the United States. The pro-Israel PACs spend approximately $5 million annually, almost all to support congressional incumbents. For them, it is money well spent. Israel in turn receives almost $4 billion annually in U.S. grants for military and economic development.[2]

More recently, however, the message to Israel has been that the United States will no longer rubber-stamp Israeli plans to simply annex the occupied territories seized by Israel during the 1967 Six-Day War. These politically charged lands include the Golan Heights, the West Bank, the Gaza Strip, and portions of the city of Jerusalem. The United States has shown that it is firmly committed to negotiation of peace settlements between Israel and its neighbors, including the Palestinians.

Statistics don't lie, but lobbyists manipulate them all the time in an effort to sway the opinions of both the public and lawmakers. One way is through the use of census-type information. The fact that there are approximately five million practicing Jews in the United States has been used to justify the large amount of foreign aid appropriated to Israel.[3] Propagandists can feel confident when they say that five million Americans are vitally concerned about the welfare of Israel. When pro-Arab lobbyists can present figures showing that six million Americans identify themselves as of Arab origin, lawmakers are equally bound to take notice.

The lobbying stakes are high—billions in annual foreign aid plus the continuing commitment of the U.S. government. Israel is the largest benefactor of America's foreign aid program. But as the American public becomes more politically aware, some of the tactics of the information branch of the American Israel Public Affairs Committee have been called into question.

THE JAPAN LOBBY

Japanese business interests have actively sought to recruit former members of Congress and attorneys with experience in dealing with Congress to represent them in Washington. So far they have been successful in helping to position Japan as the United States' chief economic rival.

The lobbyists themselves may label it Japan-bashing when government officials or members of the press lament the loss of American jobs to Asian producers of goods and components. Even the operation of businesses in the United States by overseas owners has been achieved at the expense of American businesses.

Strangely enough, American industry has sometimes helped the Japanese achieve trade dominance. Today it is almost impossible for a manufacturer to assemble an American automobile or computer hardware system (or just about any other manufactured item) without relying on parts imported from Japan—or produced domestically by Americans working for a company owned by Japanese investors.

FIVE
PUBLIC INTEREST GROUPS

Public interest groups pursue their ends by peaceful and legal means. They promote political activism, pursue legal action in court (suing to enforce compliance with the law), and conduct vigorous public information and education programs.

There are thousands of such organizations that lobby on the state and national levels, but some of the largest and most famous of them are listed here along with a brief description of their programs. They exist to serve the public's needs and welcome inquiries about their ongoing work for the improvement of society.

Greenpeace

Greenpeace is an international organization based in Amsterdam, Holland, with their U. S. headquarters in Washington, D.C. The group works on behalf of environmental issues around the world, lobbying for legislation with the governments of many countries. The organization aims to make the public aware of violations of international laws that protect various living species. The fishing industry—with its overharvesting of marine resources—has been one of their targets.

On a grassroots level, Greenpeace campaigns for funding from individuals and publishes reports about environmental issues so that it is better prepared to lobby before the U.S. Congress and governing bodies of other countries.

Viewed by many—especially those in industry—as extremists who have grabbed headlines by such tactics as cutting fishing nets and blocking the progress of vessels violating international (or moral) law, the group has been successful enough to be perceived as a threat. In fact, its vessels and personnel have themselves been the victims of organized sabotage efforts presumably financed by the fishing industry as well as by governments that refuse to comply with international treaties and environmental protection agreements.

☆ ══════ ☆

The Greenpeace organization has often used
dramatic demonstrations to gain public attention.
Here a raft carries a variety of plastic water
creatures covered with "oil" to protest proposed
oil drilling at a national marine sanctuary in Florida.

American Civil Liberties Union
One purpose of the ACLU is to defend the Bill of Rights, the basic freedoms guaranteed under the first ten amendments to

the Constitution. The organization was founded in 1920 to do just that, and to do it for *everybody*. Often the group's clients are drawn from among the less affluent members of society. The ACLU accomplishes its work through litigation in court, legislative action, and community education.

In the early 1970s, when the Watergate trials were in progress, the ACLU stepped in and stated that President Nixon would have to cooperate and turn over, as evidence, tape recordings that had been made in his office. After all, the ACLU felt, the Constitution stated that no one, not even a president, could be above the law of the land.

Common Cause

The organization was founded in 1970 to allow citizen action on a professional level that would make the government listen and respond. The group was set up to promote government measures to benefit society: public funding of presidential and congressional elections, regulation of lobbying activities, disclosure of nongovernmental sources of income by members of Congress.

Common Cause cross-lobbies with other groups in order to provide strong and cohesive coverage of important issues. The organization also attempts to educate the public about target issues. The group's *Action Manual* teaches private citizens how to write persuasive letters to congresspeople in order to get a responsive hearing for their issue. Because Common Cause tries to "keep in step," it concentrates on grassroots lobbying and sets in motion citizen response to specific legislation. Still, many people feel that the need for an organization such as Common Cause underscores the failure of their elected officials to represent them properly. Support for the lobby is tantamount to supporting an alternate government made necessary by the ineffectiveness of the Congress in Washington and of individual state legislatures.

Common Cause directs citizens to demand access to their

instruments of self-government, to demand that public officials be responsive and accountable, to advocate public interests with the same vigor that special interests lavish on their pet projects, and to watch over the actions of government as closely as the special interest groups do.

An organization like Common Cause provides political clout. Lobbying is not done at the local level but concerns itself with people-oriented issues at the state and federal levels. Common Cause does not deal with issues such as the environment or equal rights (as do other interest groups) but deals with the *procedural* ways the government is handling issues. During the 1970s, Common Cause attempted to rein in powerful lobbies by getting them to divulge their spending levels.

Common Cause also helped reform the practice of fundraising for presidential campaigns by spearheading the drive to get voters to give a dollar at tax time on their IRS forms. The House of Representatives used to have a seniority system that allowed people who had served the longest in the House access to any committee. As a result of Common Cause's efforts, all committee positions are now subject to a vote on a fair and square basis,[1] and many of the lobby's reforms have been effected at the state level as well as at the federal level.

National Urban League

Founded in 1910 and known as NUL after a few years, the organization has been determined to give African-Americans, freshly arrived in big cities from their rural homes, a chance at fair opportunities in a new and unfamiliar setting. In a time before the Civil Rights movement, the NUL fought to give African-Americans a chance at equal opportunities in employment, schooling, and housing, among other areas.

But by the 1960s, the NUL had become out-of-date and needed to address social changes and the still rampant problems of racism. NUL is now more often concerned with placing African-Americans in key positions in schools and colleges and in labor unions. Today's NUL wants strongly to eliminate racial discrimination and poverty.

League of Women Voters

The group was originally founded to help women obtain their right to vote. After that right had been achieved, the league turned its attention to getting women registered to vote.

Today the league—despite its name—is concerned with making sure that *all* Americans responsibly exercise that right. It is now divided into two organizations, the League of Women Voters Education Fund, which provides balanced nonpartisan information about public policy and election participation issues and the League of Women Voters of the United States, the membership and advocacy organization, which takes positions on public policy issues at all levels of government. The information the league provides allows voters to make intelligent choices.

National Organization for Women

NOW was founded in 1966 by a group of women who felt that American women still were being discriminated against, especially in terms of employment and wages. The establishment of NOW was spearheaded by the women's liberation movement, which had lain dormant until the publication in 1963 of Betty Friedan's book *The Feminine Mystique.* Zena Collier has written that NOW gave the women's movement "structure and strength.... It lobbies for laws that will improve the status and condition of women."[2] Most recently, NOW campaigned and lobbied for the unsuccessful Equal Rights Amendment (ERA) to the Constitution.

Sierra Club

The organization was founded originally in 1892 to preserve the Sierra Nevada, which even a century ago local residents wanted to protect from uncaring and unthinking people. In 1962 Rachel Carson's *Silent Spring* was published. Carson's exposé of the environmental chemicals that were damaging much of the country awakened many consciences. Then, in 1970, the first Earth Day brought a further awareness of the environment—and its fragile structure—to a larger group of Americans than ever before.

The Sierra Club defined its new mandate: a large-scale plan to protect the whole of the American environment. It soon

☆ ════════ ☆

Two members of an environmental group, Earth First, protest the destruction of the earth's rain forests in front of the Lincoln Memorial.

became the largest organization of environmentalists lobbying for bills concerning nature. Sierrans use lobbying to work for policies and laws that will safeguard the environment.

Nuclear waste, the damming of rivers, transportation pollution, and industrial pollution are just some of the environmental problems that the Sierra Club investigates. It rallies its members through well-written newsletters and brochures, and reaches a larger public through its strong book publishing and public relations programs.

RALPH NADER

In 1965 Ralph Nader took on the auto industry. An unknown lawyer from Connecticut, Nader had worked on a number of automobile accident cases when he began to realize that there were far too many fatalities on America's highways. His book *Unsafe at Any Speed* was an attack on the safety of cars manufactured by General Motors and, by implication, on the entire American automotive industry. Before the publication of his book, no one had heard of Nader. And even when the book was published, it didn't cause a lot of fuss—at first.

As a result of the book, Nader was soon testifying before a Senate subcommittee on automobile safety. The press picked up on these appearances. General Motors saw these newspaper articles as an attack and began to investigate Nader's private life. Some of Nader's friends were questioned and the young lawyer soon became aware that he was being followed.

NADER'S INTEGRITY

It seems that Ralph Nader's reputation for honesty has stood the test of time. Almost any money he received (both from book royalties and from settlement of the suit he brought against GM) Nader poured right back into research to support his interest in car safety. Known to be a selfless crusader, Nader has pursued a simple, at times even Spartan, lifestyle. With some of his money, he also established the Center for the Study of Responsive Law, which gave him a staff to help him continue his valuable work.

☆ ═══════ ☆

In 1993 Ralph Nader, ever the consumer advocate,
calls on President Clinton and Congress at a news conference
to tell the full costs of their NAFTA deals.

The Senate committee summoned the chairman of
General Motors, who admitted that the company had paid to
have Nader followed. A public apology from the company followed. A subsequent lawsuit brought by Nader against GM net-
ted the rebel lawyer $425,000. The Senate's interest had helped
bring Nader's cause to the public's attention and helped clear
him of any suspicion of being an eccentric or crank.

What Nader tapped into was a new American phenome-
non: citizen activism. Civil rights legislation had had some visi-
ble successes. People saw, perhaps for the first time, that massed
voices could be heard and it was in this climate that Nader's first
victories were achieved. Suddenly an ordinary citizen could
make a statement that would impact the whole country.

SIX

TODAY'S LOBBYING ISSUES

Lobbying constantly makes headlines. Almost every day, newspapers across the country describe some aspect of an issue that has forthcoming legislation.

GUN CONTROL

In the 1970s, the National Rifle Association lobbied to keep firearms—the purchase and ownership of them—legal, against a general American feeling that some guns should be banned and others should be more strongly regulated (due to the proven large percentage of homicides caused by guns). The NRA has always believed that its organization is peopled by those who use guns for sport or self-defense; their monthly newsletter goes out to more than one million readers and advocates the possession and use of firearms for nonviolent uses only.

Because of its large membership and readership, the NRA is able to count on a great number of vocal people whenever any attempt is made to ban the sale and possession of firearms. The NRA has been able to count on the support of many of our presidents, as well as members of Congress, who regularly use guns for hunting and recreational purposes. The NRA is a generous contributor to election campaign chests.

The NRA is an interest group exerting pressure in Congress and causing the holdup of bills that would prohibit the interstate sale of guns and regulate the sale of certain types of automatic weapons. Still, Congress has been successful in instituting some

The NRA is often besieged by public protests
in favor of stricter gun control.

controls over the sale of guns and the types of guns available. Both sides have employed testimony by chiefs of police and law enforcement officials in their lobbying efforts on these issues.

TOBACCO LOBBY

In 1993 lobbying organizations spent about $40 million in New York State alone on efforts in the state legislature. In New York State, the tobacco giant Philip Morris represented the largest lobbying interest, followed by lobby groups representing teachers and New York City. The tobacco industry (especially Philip Morris and R. J. Reynolds) has a great interest in lobbying. Laws regarding the taxation of cigarettes, warning labels on tobacco products, and regulation of smoking in public places all have tremendous impact on potential tobacco industry profits.

The whole smoking issue has been obscured by a lobby powerful enough and rich enough to cover up scientific evidence that the nicotine in tobacco is an addictive drug and that cigarettes may contain traces of more than 600 chemicals, many of them harmful and proven carcinogenic (or cancer causing).

On March 16, 1994, the *New York Times* ran this headline: PHILIP MORRIS TOPS LIST OF LOBBYING SPENDERS IN NEW YORK.

"In all," the article reported, "1,142 organizations, from private corporations to public authorities, paid a record $38.5 million last year for lobbying efforts to influence state legislation, an 11 percent increase over 1992, the annual report from the New York Temporary State Commission on Lobbying said."[1]

The key phrase here is "lobbying efforts to influence state legislation." Why is Philip Morris spending so much money? Simply because smoking has become both a medical and a social issue. In the last fifteen years, the number of smokers in the United States has dwindled alarmingly, according to Philip Morris. Without smokers to buy cigarettes, the tobacco industry has suffered. So Philip Morris, not even among the top ten spenders in 1992, suddenly decided in 1993 to spend money to hire lobbyists to woo legislators on the company's behalf. Philip Morris and R. J. Reynolds—and other cigarette manufacturers as well—feel that their views need to be heard.

The smoking issue is now at the federal level. In 1994 legislation was pending that would put additional taxes on the sale of cigarettes. Again, cigarette manufacturers are worried that these taxes could put the cost of a pack of cigarettes out of the reach of many customers. Also at stake is the composition of a single cigarette. Is nicotine an addictive substance, as seven tobacco company representatives denied in April of 1994 when they appeared before Congress?[2]

HEALTH CARE REFORM

One of today's most important lobbying issues, health care has become a lobbying free-for-all. Big business questions who will pick up the tab. Employee groups are left wondering what the plan will cost and whether their benefits will improve or deteriorate. And the insurance and pharmaceutical industries are fearful that government regulation will put a cap on their profits.

The grassroots phenomenon is playing a large part in the health care debates. The Health Insurance Association of America has "set up an '800' number and telephone bank to get out their message that the Clinton plan would mean higher insurance premiums and fewer health care choices for consumers,"[3] according to a report in the *New York Times*. So many people are involved at local levels that "members of Congress say they don't have the time to schedule all the face-to-face

☆ ══════════ ☆

The health care debate has given rise to protests for and
against various issues involved in the proposed legislation.

meetings that have been requested from dance therapists, masseurs, chiropractors, and podiatrists."[4]

Health care is one of the major industries in the United States. It employs millions and touches everyone's lives. But there has been such rampant growth in costs that the need for reform is obvious. As health care affects nearly everyone, it has become an emotionally and politically charged issue. Health care is literally a life or death situation, and talk of "rationing" available health care services has everyone up in arms. Still, roughly forty million Americans currently have no health care insurance coverage.

BREAST CANCER

Like AIDS, the issue of breast cancer is a major one for the American public, especially women. In 1993, *Time* magazine reported that "breast-cancer victims and their supporters have become a powerful political force over the past year."[5]

But a battle is looming that questions whether or not the money that lobbying brings in will be used properly. What kind of research will be done? Mammogram tests have proven effective in diagnosing incidences of breast cancer only in women over age fifty, so the National Cancer Institute is recommending that younger women should "no longer be given routine mammograms unless there is some reason . . . to suspect a higher-than-normal risk."[6] But many women are upset by this pronouncement—they don't believe that enough research has been done to arrive at this conclusion.

SEVEN
THE CHANGING
FACE OF LOBBYING

POLITICAL ACTION COMMITTEES

There are powerful external forces that act upon our elected government officials. These include special interest groups, lobbies, and political action committees (PACs). All of these forces affect and influence the policies and actions of the federal government.

PACs are a very recent development in American politics, not much heard of before the 1980s. They are large and powerful groups. The stick they wield is often financial. PACs can offer support to election campaigns and can threaten to work against candidates by supporting the opposition. In 1974 there were about 600 PACs. By 1990 there were more than 4,200.[1]

PACs channel their energies (and money) directly into electing candidates who will best represent their interests. PACs are often one part of an overall lobbying or interest group plan. PACs spend big money. In recent campaigns, 70 to 80 percent of PAC money has gone to support incumbents in their reelection campaigns.

CLINTON, HIGH TECH, AND GRASSROOTS LOBBYING

President Clinton has often denounced lobbying, but the influence-peddling industry has grown rampantly since the Reagan and Bush administrations. Ironically, under Clinton, lobbying continues to flourish. *Time* magazine reports that some of

Clinton's appointees "have been accused of influence peddling, notably Secretary of Commerce Ron Brown."[2] Clinton has tried to put a lid on senior members of his administration; they may not become lobbyists for a period of five years after they leave office.

An ironic twist to Clinton's position is that his proposed health care reform program will be the cause for even more lobbying in the future. Those affected include "big business, small business, insurers, unions, doctors, nurses, the elderly, the poor— just about every group well organized enough to employ a lobbyist."[3]

In 1993 the *New York Times* reported that "Over the last several years, lobbyists have been turning away from the direct approach in favor of 'grass roots' strategies. Largely gone are the days of corridor buttonholing and lavish lunches to 'persuade' legislators. Now lobbyists are going directly to the American public."[4]

The efficiency of lobbyists' efforts has improved; lobbying has gone high-tech, with computerized databases, mailing lists, and other technological advances. States one *New York Times* journalist, Michael Wines, "Grassroots lobbying—from organized letter-writing campaigns to computer-driven efforts to whip up voter opinion back in the home districts—has become the preferred way of pressuring Government officials and lawmakers to make or change policies."[5]

Late in 1993, Joel Brinkley of the *New York Times* reported on a new trend. Lobbyists are now showing television advertisements that promote their side of an argument. "That approach was used only rarely before now because of the tremendous cost. But once industry decides it is willing to spend the money, others find they have little choice."[6] At the ends of the ads are toll-free numbers for convinced viewers to use. "New telemarketing companies answer these calls, and transfer the callers directly to the offices of the appropriate congressmen."[7]

The American Trucking Association used fax machines

until it found its members were swamped with pieces of paper. "So this month the truckers began using a new satellite network connecting the Washington headquarters to affiliates in every state. Now . . . the president of the Association can appear on television monitors in affiliate offices nationwide and rally his members to action."[8]

"'These developing technologies—like computerized grass roots—combined with enormous resources, are overwhelming the system,' complained Fred Wertheimer, head of Common Cause, one of the first organizations to use modern grass-roots lobbying."[9]

CHANGING LAWS FOR LOBBYISTS

It is becoming clear to those concerned that "the laws and rules have not kept up with the explosive changes in the way lobbyists actually wield influence now."[10]

"The 1989 Ethics in Government Act bars top Congressional aides from lobbying their old offices for one year after leaving Government. Elected officials are barred for a year from lobbying anywhere on Capitol Hill."[11]

Lobbyists are trying to kill a clause in a bill that President Clinton signed into law in the summer of 1993. Simply put, the legislation bars taxpayers from writing off the costs of efforts to influence legislation in the federal and state governments. It also prohibits deducting the costs of any effort to influence actions by the federal government's most senior officials. The law allowing such deductions dates back to 1962, the Kennedy era, but it has many loopholes.

"But the beleaguered lobbyists still argue that they have been unfairly singled out by lawmakers who believe that in the current anti-Washington climate, only God loves a lobbyist, and that may be a reach even for Him."[12]

EIGHT
LOBBYING IN
THE HEADLINES

In assessing the need for reform, Senator Frank Lautenberg, a Democrat from New Jersey, said in the course of a news release: "The public doesn't trust Congress to do their work." Dear to the hearts of senators have been the free trips, the skiing and golf vacations, the hearty lunches, and country club memberships. Lobbying has come a long way from the out-and-out bribery that characterized it in the nineteenth century.

The right to lobby is validated in the Constitution. However, from time to time perceived abuses of the system have led to reforms in the way lobbying is conducted. Today lobbying is fairly scrupulous and not openly corrupt. Laws and regulations have been enacted to prevent bribery and blatant abuse. Watchdog agencies in the government and special interest groups keep a keen eye on legislators, lobbyists, and their activities.

But even with significant reforms, lobbying will still play an important role. Lobbyists will continue to have a strong impact on (1) whom the parties nominate at their political conventions, (2) which candidates receive election support, and (3) which members of Congress are named to key committees.

If people think lobbying is not a relevant issue for today—and tomorrow—they should take a look at the *New York Times*. On May 12, 1994, not one but two front-page articles featured stories about the changing face of lobbying.

One headline read SENATE APPROVES BILL TO BAN GIFTS FROM LOBBYISTS. The substance of the story revealed that the Senate had voted 95 to 4 to "prohibit lawmakers from accepting gifts, meals and recreational travel from lobbyists or anyone except family members and genuine friends."[1] This only reinforced a similar, earlier vote in the House of Representatives. Part of the bill also would require lobbyists to disclose how much money they spend and their methods of working.

The second front-page article, two columns away, dealt with another pervasive change in lobbying: the fact that many of the people who are entering the field of lobbying already have strong political ties and an insider's knowledge of how the system works. EX-AIDE IS NOW LOBBYIST WITH WHITE HOUSE TIES begins this article.

The article notes that Betsey Wright, a "new" lobbyist, is a staunch Clinton "adviser and confidante."[2] While many other lobbyists work diligently to get the ear of someone influential, here's a person who already has *entrée* to the top office in the land. It's not a totally new phenomenon; both Reagan and Bush had "friends" who were also lobbyists. But during his election campaign, Clinton made fun of those "special" relationships and pledged that the same thing wouldn't happen when he became president. And now it has.

A source states that "government service has become required training for almost every aspiring lobbyist—and lobbying, far from scorned, has become a routine second career for bureaucrats at all levels of government."[3] Who knows the ins and outs of government better than a veteran politician or a seasoned bureaucrat?

Lobbyists may have to regroup their forces. At different times, they have been more active and more powerful, but in all periods of American history lobbyists have been a very real presence in American government. But thanks to regulations, their influence has been controlled and their roles have been more carefully defined. Even with its changing face, lobbying is a concept that is here to stay.

SOURCE NOTES

Introduction

1. John Diamond, "Clinton Lobbying Spares C-17 Transport Project," *Schenectady Gazette*, May 25, 1994, D6.

One

1. Milton Meltzer, *American Politics: How It Really Works* (New York: Morrow Junior Books, 1989), 117.

Two

1. Fred J. Cook, *Lobbying in American Politics* (New York: Franklin Watts, 1976), 33.

2. *Encyclopedia Britannica*, Vol. 14 (1947), 259.

3. Cook, *Lobbying in American Politics*, 65 ff.

Three

1. Lawrence I. Barrett, "A Lobbyist's Paradise, *Time*, November 1, 1993, 36–37.

2. G. William Domhoff, *Who Rules America?* (Englewood Cliffs, N.J.: Prentice-Hall, 1967), 112.

3. Barrett, "A Lobbyist's Paradise," 36–37

4. Ibid.

5. Ibid

6. Meltzer, *American Politics*, 108.

Four

1. Stephen Engelberg with Martin Tolchin, "Foreigners Find New Ally in U.S. Industry," *New York Times*, November 2, 1993, A1.

2. Christopher Hitchens, "Settled: Why Bush Will Yield to Israel and the Lobby," *Harper's*, January 1992, 57.

3. Ibid.

Five

1. Zena Collier, *Seven for the People: Public Interest Groups at Work* (New York: Julian Messner, 1979), 50.

2. Ibid, 112.

Six

1. Ian Fisher, "Philip Morris Tops List of Lobbying Spenders in New York," *New York Times*, March 16, 1994, A20.

2. Phillip J. Hilts, "Tobacco Chiefs Say Cigarettes Aren't Addictive," *New York Times*, April 15, 1994, A1.

3. Clifford Kraus, "Lobbyists of Every Stripe Turn to the Grass Roots on Health Care," *New York Times*, September 24, 1993, A1.

4. Ibid

5. Janice M. Horowitz, "Breast Cancer Priorities," *Time*, November 1, 1992, 14.

6. Ibid.

Seven

1. Bob Bernotas, *The Federal Government: How It Works* (New York: Chelsea House, 1990), 112.

2. Barrett, "A Lobbyist's Paradise," 37.

3. Kraus, "Lobbyists of Every Stripe," A1.

4. Joel Brinkley, "Lobbying Tactics: Lobbying Goes High Tech," *New York Times*, November 1, 1993, A1.

5. Michael Wines, "For New Lobbyists, It's What They Know, Not Who They Know," *New York Times*, November 3, 1993.

6. Brinkley, "Lobbying Tactics," A1 ff.

7. Ibid.

8. Ibid.

9. Ibid.

10. Ibid.

11. Ibid.

12. Michael Wines, "Lobbyists Scramble to Kill a Clause That's About Them," *New York Times*, August 27, 1993, A1

Eight

1. "Senate Approves Bill to Ban Gifts from Lobbyists," *New York Times*, May 12, 1994, A1.

2. "Ex-Aide Is Now Lobbyist with White House Ties," *New York Times*, May 12, 1994, A1.

3. Wines, "For New Lobbyists," B14.

buttonholing lobbying conducted by one-on-one direct conversations with legislators.

compromise an agreement reached, usually by two or more sides.

constituents citizens represented by an elected official.

democracy government by the people.

faction a group representing one side of an issue.

grassroots lobbying lobbying done by and among masses of ordinary citizens.

muckraking journalism that uncovers and exposes wrongdoings, scandals, and abuses in government and/or industry.

patronage the power to make appointments on a basis other than merit.

pluralism the concept that society represents diverse interest groups.

political action committee (PAC) an interest group organized primarily to support political campaigns.

pressure groups interest groups that exert strong pressure on legislators and government officials.

propaganda information (often biased) designed to sway public opinion.

public interest group a group of people who band together to seek a common goal. Usually, the goal is one of interest to the greatest number of people.

special interest group people who band together, using legal means, to pursue a common end. The interest group is usually concerned with a very specific goal that may not be of interest to many people.

spoils system (as "spoils of war,") the idea that winning an election gives the victor license to plunder.

☆ ════════ **FURTHER READING** ════════ ☆

Books

Asbell, Bernard. *The Senate Nobody Knows*. Garden City, N.Y.: Doubleday, 1978.

Ashworth, William. *Under the Influence: Congress, Lobbies, and the American Pork-Barrel System*. New York: Hawthorn and Dutton, 1981.

Bernotas, Bob. *The Federal Government: How it Works*. New York: Chelsea House, 1990.

Berry, Jeffrey M. *Lobbying for the People: The Political Behavior of Public Interest Groups*. Princeton, N.J.: Princeton University Press, 1977.

Birnbaum, Jeffrey H. *The Lobbyists: How Influence Peddlers Get Their Way in Washington*. New York: Times Books, 1992.

Cigler, Allan J., and Burdett A. Loomis, eds. *Interest Group Politics*, 3d ed. Washington, D.C.: Congressional Quarterly Press, 1991.

Collier, Zena. *Seven for the People: Public Interest Groups at Work*. New York: Julian Messner, 1979.

Congressional Ethics, 2d ed. Washington, D.C.: Congressional Quarterly, 1980.

Cook, Fred J. *Lobbying in American Politics*. New York: Franklin Watts, 1976.

Domhoff, G. William. *Who Rules America?* Englewood Cliffs, N.J.: Prentice-Hall, 1967.

How Congress Works. Washington, D.C.: Congressional Quarterly, 1983.

Meltzer, Milton. *American Politics: How It Really Works*. New York: Morrow Junior Books, 1989.

Pertschuk, Michael. *Giant Killers*. New York: W. W. Norton & Company, 1986.

Ritchie, Donald A. *The Senate*. New York: Chelsea House, 1988.

Sagstetter, Karen. *Lobbying*. New York: Franklin Watts, 1978.

Wolpe, Bruce C. *Lobbying Congress: How the System Works*. Washington, D.C.: Congressional Quarterly, 1991.

Periodicals

Hitchens, Christopher. "Settled: Why Bush Will Yield to Israel and the Lobby." *Harper's*, January 1992.

New York Times, August 27, 1993–May 12, 1994.

DATE DUE

			PRINTED IN U.S.A.
GAYLORD			